Imagining a New World:
An Advent Devotional

by Terri Hord Owens

chalice
press

Saint Louis, Missouri

ChalicePress.com

Print: 9780827216792
EPUB: 9780827216808
EPDF: 9780827216815

Printed in the United States of America

CONTENTS

INTRODUCTION

2020 has been a challenging year in the life of our families, the church, and the world. The global COVID-19 pandemic has brought changes, sickness, death, and disruption unlike anything in most of our lifetimes. We simply could not have anticipated these circumstances, and as I write, we do not really know what the world will look like in Advent 2020. While we miss what was, we realize that the world will never be quite the same again. As followers of Jesus Christ, we are now called to imagine a new world, and who we will be as church in it.

On February 23, 2020, I gave the "State of the Church" address to the General Board of the Christian Church (Disciples of Christ). I told the board that we must have the courage to imagine not only a new church for a new world, but how we as church could help to shape that world. I said we needed to give ourselves permission to change, to let go of processes, structures, and even practices, emboldening ourselves to try and explore new understandings of ministry. Even more importantly, Jesus called for change in his ministry on earth. The early church itself was born in the midst of radical change: crucifixion, resurrection, and Pentecost were all moments of massive disruption for those earliest followers of Christ. Finally, I said, we must let go of the fear of what will happen when we do change. God has not given us a spirit of fear but of love, power, and confidence.

Little did I know that only three weeks later the COVID-19 pandemic would hand us a new world. Some of us began working remotely. Congregations could not worship in person, and we had to learn how to worship, care for, and connect with each other in new ways. We have had to re-evaluate the use and value of our buildings. We have had to find ways to connect and sustain relationships on Zoom, Facebook, and YouTube. We have been unable to care for the sick and comfort the bereaved with our physical presence. Celebrations of life have been re-imagined because we cannot gather. We have had to name the added stress and exhaustion that life in a pandemic has brought to us and to focus on self-care for ourselves and others. Most importantly, we have had to call on God to teach us, guide us, encourage us, and help us imagine new ways to live out God's love and witness for justice and peace from beyond our four walls.

In each of these devotionals, I have tried to invite us into a space of courageous and prophetic imagination. When we embrace Jesus as God in our midst, who then must we be? How then must we love? What then must we do? Walter Brueggemann reminds us: "the imagination must come before the implementation." As you enter into this season of anticipation and expectation, may the Spirit feed your heart, mind and spirit as we imagine a new church in this new world, called by God, grounded in love, and enlightened by the Word.

First Week of Advent

The Urgency of Now

Read Isaiah 64:1–9

O that you would tear open the heavens and come down,
  so that the mountains would quake at your presence—
as when fire kindles brushwood
  and the fire causes water to boil—
to make your name known to your adversaries,
  so that the nations might tremble at your presence. (Isaiah 64:1–2)

Isaiah speaks to God on behalf of a people who have run out of time, a people who need God to show up—NOW! Living under the oppression of Rome, holding fast to the promise of a Messiah, they are impatient for the promise to be fulfilled. They want God to show up in ways that would cause fire to burn wood and boil water! They need God to move as never before, and the prophet calls for God to do it in ways that people will take notice.

Like the Israelites, many communities today live constantly on the edge of enough, marginalized and living with constant and multiple traumas of poverty and oppression. We impatiently anticipate solutions to our problems: more money, a new job, a safe home, protection for our loved ones. If you have life-challenging problems, you need solutions today. If you are in a burning building, you need the firefighters to break through walls, shatter windows, and knock down doors. There are times when we simply need God to move—now.

I feel the prophet's urgency for our world today. Do what you have to do, Lord—tear open the heavens, break down the door—come down! Now! Let us embrace the urgency of this moment in our society, anticipating and expecting God to move as only God can. In this unprecedented time, we need something new that we have never had before, and Lord, we need you now!

Prayer: Tear open our hearts, set our souls afire, mold and make us to be the reflection of your love, working boldly to imagine and create a new world—now. Come through now, O God. In the name of Jesus, Amen.

What Will God Do through You?

Read Isaiah 64:1–9

Yet, O Lord, you are our Father [Mother];
we are the clay, and you are our potter;
we are all the work of your hand. (Isaiah 64:8)

Wouldn't it be wonderful if we had a clear layout of God's plan for our lives? We are eager to take assessment tests to learn more about our personality, temperament, gifts, strengths, and weaknesses. It is usually not so much that we don't know ourselves, but rather that we want some kind of clear sign that who we understand ourselves to be is truly who we are. More importantly, we want to know if who we are is what God has planned.

Having called out to God to act, the prophet acknowledges that we must yet be yielded to God's creative power. Yes, yielded, being ready to be used in the kin(g)dom of God in ways that weren't a part of our own plans. God can use every experience we've had along the way to bring us into a way of being and serving. God can show us how every step, every stumble, every turn in the road along the way can be used to equip for this moment. In this season when we welcome the new light, may you see how God has led, and remember that God will keep.

Prayer: Mold us, make us, O God, so that we may have courage to step forth into new ways of being your people. Give us the courage to yield ourselves to new shapes and patterns that can be reflections of your love in the world. Amen.

Thanking God for You

Read 1 Thessalonians 3:9–13

How can we thank God enough for you in return for all the joy that we feel before our God because of you? Night and day we pray most earnestly that we may see you face to face and restore whatever is lacking in your faith. Now may our God and Father himself and our Lord Jesus direct our way to you. And may the Lord make you increase and abound in love for one another and for all, just as we abound in love for you. And may he so strengthen your hearts in holiness that you may be blameless before our God and Father at the coming of our Lord Jesus with all his saints. (1 Thessalonians 3:9–13)

As I am completing the writing of this devotional, the entire world is in quarantine because of the COVID-19 pandemic crisis. We find that we have no choice but to adapt to using technology to stay connected. We are gathering on FaceTime and Zoom, struggling to create meaning in these digital spaces. We have now celebrated a Palm Sunday and Easter in these isolated rhythms, boldly declaring "Hosanna" and "He is Risen!" as we responded in online worship services. We miss each other.

Paul's longing for the Thessalonians is palpable, but he is not just missing their physical fellowship. Out of his love, he is praying for them. He wants them to grow, to love each other lavishly, fully. As we live into being church in this new world, now forever changed by COVID-19, I hope you are praying for us all to love more like Jesus. The selfishness that too often invades communal life, even in church, must give way to an abundance of love and grace. May our living into a new love and gratitude for one another light our pathway to the kingdom of God.

Prayer: Lord, may our love for one another strengthen us as we build your beloved community. Now more than ever, fill our hearts with thanksgiving for each one you have created and called your own. In Jesus' name, Amen.

God Is Faithful

Read 1 Corinthians 1:3–9

God is faithful; by him you were called into the fellowship of his Son, Jesus Christ our Lord. (1 Corinthians 1:9)

What do you mean when you say, "God is faithful"? For some, it is just a polite way to respond to a compliment, or a way of acknowledging God's goodness when we have received material blessings. It is often our response once we have been through a tough time. But what does it mean to say, "God is faithful" when we are in the midst of difficult circumstances? What grounds our ability to declare God's faithfulness in hard times?

Paul speaks to the church in Corinth, encouraging them in the midst of persecution. Enduring hardship is not desirable nor should it be considered necessary as some sort of badge for righteous nobility. Suffering is, however, part of our human existence. Paul gives thanks that their testimony about Jesus has not been shaken by difficult situations. Our faith in God must begin with what we believe about God. If we believe that God's love is limitless and all-encompassing, then any attempt to limit that love diminishes who God is. And if we believe that God is ever-present and that God's essence is love, any theology that would separate God from God's creation diminishes God. I cannot embrace a God whom humankind can limit or diminish. I believe that God is limitless, ever-loving, and all-encompassing. And because I believe that, I can firmly say, "God is faithful."

Prayer: Thank you, God, for reminding me you are never limited by circumstance or human interpretation. You are faithful. Amen.

Walking in the Light of God

Read Isaiah 2:1–5

He shall judge between the nations,
and shall arbitrate for many peoples;
they shall beat their swords into plowshares,
and their spears into pruning hooks;
nation shall not lift up sword against nation,
neither shall they learn war any more.
O house of Jacob,
come, let us walk in the light
of the Lord! (Isaiah 2:4–5)

When humans are deprived of light, our sense of well-being is adversely affected. When communities face systemic injustice, their physical and mental security is traumatized and diminished. Without the light of hope, and the establishment of justice, such social violence can stunt our human capacity to thrive.

Isaiah paints a vivid picture of a place where God dwells, in the highest of mountains, lofty and spectacular. It is not just a beautiful place but sacred space, where justice reigns and where people will seek to be like God. Nations will no longer fight, and they will use the resources once used for war to build peace among all peoples. This vision is cast for a people who have known exile, oppression, and defeat. Isaiah knows that the vision of this powerful and just God is the only hope that can break through their darkness.

Only the light of a loving God can give us such a hopeful vision. Only when we seek to be like God, to love like Jesus, can we take the systems of this world, so long used to perpetuate injustice, and build a world where all can thrive, where all have enough.

Prayer: Lift our heads toward you, O God, that we may arise from the depths of injustice, ready to walk together in your light, building a world where all are loved, and where all have enough. In the name of Jesus, Amen.

The House of the Lord

Read Psalm 122

I was glad when they said to me,
  "Let us go to the house of the Lord!" (Psalm 122:1)

Psalm 122:1 was one of the first Bible verses I learned as a child. Church folk were excited to be in the sanctuary to praise God, and this verse was used as the first line of many a testimony offered during the devotional period. In the African American community, "the house of the Lord" represented not only a place where one felt the presence of God but also a place where we were fully in charge, a building we owned and could use as we wished.

The Jewish people were bereft when the Temple was destroyed. They lived for generations without being able to worship there, at times not even being able to enter Jerusalem. The COVID-19 pandemic kept us from our traditional holy spaces. We have embraced the truth that wherever we encounter the Holy is sacred space. Any table around which all are welcome is the Lord's Table. Any spot from which the gospel is preached is sacred. The house of the Lord can be constituted in cyberspace. Gratefully we enter the sacred spaces of our making, lifting voices and hearts to praise a God who cannot be contained.

Prayer: O Holy One, may we make space within and all around us for your presence among us. In Jesus' name, Amen.

Time to Wake Up

Read Romans 13:11–14

Besides this, you know what time it is, how it is now the moment for you to wake from sleep. For salvation is nearer to us now than when we became believers. (Romans 13:11)

To be "woke" in our contemporary vernacular is to be aware of the injustices in our society and to be vigilant in fighting against them. To not be "woke" is to be oblivious to systems that create inequity, or to fail to resist them even if you are aware. To see injustice and not try to fight it is perhaps the height of selfishness that seeks only to preserve one's own comfort and privilege. "Woke" people are impatient people who do not believe that justice can wait. They live into what Dr. Martin Luther King Jr. called "the fierce urgency of now."

Paul called the church in Rome to "wake from sleep." The kingdom was closer than it had ever been, he reminded them, so it was more important than ever that they be examples of the power of Jesus' love. Followers of Christ cannot afford to be asleep on the watch for justice, for love compels us to live into Jesus' message of peace and hope for all. The urgency of the new world proclaimed by Jesus compels us to wake up and get to work. Love demands our all as never before. It is past time to wake up.

Prayer: Lord, give us courage to wake up, stand up, and show up for the reign of God to which you have called us. May our living into your love bring your reign to us now. May it be so, Amen.

Second Week of Advent

A Model for Our Movement

Read Isaiah 11:1–10

They will not hurt or destroy
on all my holy mountain;
for the earth will be full of the knowledge of the LORD
as the waters cover the sea. (Isaiah 11:9)

This familiar passage describes what is known as "the peaceable kingdom," what the world would look like once the Messiah came. There are important elements of this kin[g]dom that are crucial to the movement that followers of Jesus seek to build:

- The spirit of the Lord is present. (Isaiah 11:2) Without the spirit, there can be no movement.

- We cannot judge by appearance or by what we hear, but we must decide with equity for the sake of all. (Isaiah 11:3–4)

- Righteousness and faithfulness are what grounds us. (Isaiah 11:5)

- Those who are natural or human-made enemies can coexist and live together when they understand and respect each other's stories and ways. The most vulnerable are protected. (Isaiah 11:6–8)

- The kin[g]dom of God, this peaceable kingdom, will be full of the knowledge of God, and we will seek only to uplift, not to hurt or destroy. (Isaiah 11:9)

The knowledge of the Lord begins with spiritual disciplines of prayer, biblical study, and theological reflection. We must give ourselves permission to see spiritual practices as a necessary foundation for our beloved community. From that grounding can come the courage to imagine a new world, the permission to change and let things go, and the freedom from fear of the change that must come. Let us begin.

Prayer: O Holy One, draw us closer to you. May your spirit fill us, and may we love as you love. Give us respect for all we encounter, and help us commit our lives to this movement, to shaping a new world, guided by your love and peace. Amen.

Comfort My People

Read Isaiah 40:1–11

Comfort, O comfort my people,
  says your God.
Speak tenderly to Jerusalem,
  and cry to her
that she has served her term,
  that her penalty is paid,
that she has received from the Lord's *hand*
  double for all her sins. (Isaiah 40:1-2)

Every child learning to ride a bike inevitably falls. As parents, we want our children to learn how to move past the falls, to get up and try again. We comfort them, to be sure, acknowledging the scrapes and scratches, giving hugs and kisses to make them feel better. We want them to know that despite the fall, they can succeed. We do not want them to stay on the ground. We do not comfort to allow them to be comfortable on the ground, but rather to give them the love and confidence to get up and keep trying.

God's comfort is beyond any comfort we can offer each other. In the midst of all of life's difficulties, the words of Isaiah must be heard as the deep commitment of God to give us the confidence we need to keep moving. Jesus can wipe away every tear, can work it out, to be sure. But we are comforted not so we can simply be comfortable. We are comforted so that we can become more than our situations suggest. Those who have found God's comfort are charged to "get you up to a high mountain,/ O Zion, herald of good tidings; /lift up your voice with strength,/... lift it up, do not fear; /say to the cities of Judah, /"Here is your God!" (Isaiah 40: 9). Those who have known the Lord's comfort must proclaim the Lord's goodness, full of hope, free from fear.

Prayer: Thank you, gracious God, for your comfort that surrounds us. May we arise from our darkest moments prepared to lift up our voices without fear to proclaim your goodness. Amen.

I Am Confident

Read Philippians 1:3–11

I am confident of this, that the one who began a good work among you will bring it to completion by the day of Jesus Christ. (Philippians 1:6)

Full disclosure: Philippians 1:6 is my personal theme scripture. As a second career divinity school student who worked full-time, then became a bi-vocational pastor, I spent many years wrestling with discerning God's will for my life. That struggle is familiar to many, I know. I used to ask God why God hadn't made it clearer to me earlier in my life, so that I might have gone straight onto a path toward ordained ministry. But I now understand that my career experiences prepared me in important ways for the ministry to which I am called. I wouldn't be here if I hadn't gone on that journey.

Paul writes to an early church in Philippi, speaking encouragement to them in the midst of struggle. Maybe their own vision for their ministry was not shaping up as they'd hoped. Paul's prayer for them is that they may grow in the knowledge and love of Jesus Christ, and then determine what is best for them to do. Why? So that they may be effective witnesses of the gospel of Jesus Christ. Paul's confidence is not in the Philippians, but rather in God's ability to complete the work God started in them. I have confidence, not so much in you, but in God to complete the work that God has begun in every one of us.

Prayer: Faithful God, hear our hearts cry out to walk in the confidence of your ability to do abundantly above all that we could ask or imagine. We can't wait to see how you will accomplish your purposes in us. Amen.

Give Them Your Justice

Read Psalm 72:1–7,18–19

May he defend the cause of the poor of the people,
give deliverance to the needy,
and crush the oppressor. (Psalm 72:4)

The COVID-19 crisis has laid bare the pervasive inequities and injustices in our society that have been present for decades. Despite the advocacy of faithful people, we still find that our country does not prioritize the needs of the poor and oppressed. Amid the growing count of sick and dying, and those impacted financially, we know that the poor and marginalized are suffering most. It is clear that we must continue our fight to ensure that we all have jobs, healthcare, food, and shelter. We must be in prayer for those elected and appointed officials whose decisions impact our world. Whether we agree with them or not, as followers of Christ we must be in continual prayer that they may love mercy and act justly.

What the psalmist seeks is the peace, mercy, and justice of God. He places this king in a circle of prayer, invoking God's wisdom and grace to be shown through the leader. Our nation and world are divided because of those whose decisions are in conflict with the command to love our neighbor. To usher in a new world, that peaceable kin[g]dom where all have enough, we must pray for wisdom as we select leaders, then hold them accountable as they lead.

Prayer: Dear Lord, may our leaders have your heart for justice, may they defend and deliver the poor and needy, may oppression be crushed in our midst. Give them your heart, and grant them your wisdom as they serve. In Jesus' name we pray, Amen.

Welcome One Another

Read Romans 15:4–13

Welcome one another, therefore, just as Christ has welcomed you, for the glory of God. (Romans 15:7)

"We are Disciples of Christ, a movement for wholeness in a fragmented world. As part of the one body of Christ, we welcome all to the Lord's Table as God has welcomed us." – Disciples of Christ Identity Statement

Our denomination has come to deeply embrace our identity statement. While we work for wholeness, we are living in a fragmented, divided world. We declare that we are Christians, but not the only ones, and that we are part of the one body of Christ. Most profoundly, we welcome all to the Lord's Table, not just because it's the hospitable thing to do, but because God has welcomed us. Disciples are diverse in so many ways. The beauty of our movement is the unity that we seek among all who profess Jesus as Lord and Savior. It is hard work to engage with people when you disagree, especially when their experiences and perspectives are much different than your own. As my friend Julia Middleton would say, we must recognize that none of us is the "benchmark for all people."

In Romans 15, Paul reminds the church in Rome that they must welcome one another, just as Christ has welcomed them. Not because it feels good, but for the glory of God. I want to be a part of a church where others will look at how we love, how we engage, how we respect one another's differences, and say, " how do they walk together even when they disagree?" This is the most profound witness to the gospel of Jesus Christ that we can make.

Prayer: Loving Lord, may we welcome all just as you have welcomed us. May the Lord's Table be only the beginning of radical hospitality throughout the fellowship of believers. May it be so. Amen.

Actively Waiting

Read 2 Peter 3:8–15a

Since all these things are to be dissolved in this way, what sort of persons ought you to be in leading lives of holiness and godliness, waiting for and hastening the coming of the day of God? (2 Peter 3:11–12a)

Waiting has to be one of the most challenging things for humans to do. Some of us are uncomfortable with the unknown and like to have things mapped out far in advance. Others are more spontaneous and prefer to respond in the moment to whatever comes. Many of us are afraid to put all our eggs in one basket, so we wait with only half-hearted hope.

The earliest Christians lived in expectation of Jesus' return—any day, they hoped. As time went on, it became clear that they didn't know exactly when Jesus would return. Paul encourages them to consider how their active living according to the teaching of Jesus can help them (and the world) prepare for the coming of the day of God, the new world that Jesus will usher in.

If we are indeed to usher in a new world, where the church is relevant, life-giving, and transformative, what kind of people must we be? What kind of lives must we live? We must actively stand up, show up, love, give, and bear witness to Christ through advocacy for peace and justice. We must not be found sitting idly by. We are the change we seek, and the ones who will help to shape the new world of God's reign.

Prayer: Lord, we eagerly await your return. Help us to live so that even now the world is shaped in your image, ready to be the new world of God's reign. Even so, come, Lord Jesus. Amen.

Listening for God

Read Psalm 85:1-2, 8-13

Let me hear what God the Lord will speak,
for he will speak peace to his people,
to his faithful, to those who turn to him in their hearts. (Psalm 85:8)

The world of social media has created a class of people known as "influencers." From beauty advice, fitness, cooking, and crafts to politics and religion, there are those who cultivate "followers." As you read comments on various social media platforms, these followers hold the influencers in high regard, and often create a very personal bond with them. Followers are encouraged not only to subscribe or follow the page but to turn on notifications so that they will know when new material has been posted. One can become an influencer with thousands, tens of thousands, or hundreds of thousands of followers, but not be known to the more traditional media outlets of TV and radio. What are the influencers talking about? Is it that important? How do we decide who influences us, and to whom we will give direct access to our hearts and minds?

A spiritual foundation is essential if we are to live as part of the one body of Christ. Our own scriptural engagement and reflection, guided by the Holy Spirit, helps us to hear the voice of God and to follow the teachings of Jesus Christ. Music, books, devotionals, and other resources can also play a large part in feeding our spirits and preparing us to hear the voice of God. Be sure that you take great care in deciding what voices to listen to, and what you allow to influence your thinking, your spirit, and your journey of faith. Listen closely and carefully to hear from God.

Prayer: Gracious God, draw us closer so that we may hear from you. Nourish our spirits, guide us with your wisdom, and open our hearts to commune with you all along our journey. In Jesus' name, Amen.

Third Week of Advent

A Ministry of Liberation

Read Isaiah 61:1–4, 8-11

The spirit of the Lord God is upon me, / because the Lord has anointed me ;/ he has sent me to bring good news to the oppressed, / to bind up the brokenhearted ,/ to proclaim liberty to the captives, / and release to the prisoners; / to proclaim the year of the Lord's favor, / and the day of vengeance of our God; / to comfort all who mourn; / to provide for those who mourn in Zion— / to give them a garland instead of ashes, / the oil of gladness instead of mourning /, the mantle of praise instead of a faint spirit. (Isaiah 61:1–3)

The earthly ministry of Jesus was a real disruption to his contemporaries. Those who were waiting for a kingly deliverer instead saw this humble carpenter who embraced a bold calling: to minister to the oppressed, the brokenhearted, the captives, the prisoners, and those who mourn. This text from Isaiah 61 is what Jesus famously read in his home congregation, a reading recorded in Luke 4. Many societies have sought to justify the inequities and injustices they promote by misusing biblical texts. Here, however, we find that Jesus aligns himself with the gospel of liberation. That is his calling, and he stands with so many whom society has cast aside.

If we are to imagine a new world, and a new church to shape and inhabit that world, we must look for the opportunity for liberation at every turn. Jesus named his calling, and as his followers we must find ourselves where Jesus would be. By naming liberation as a core of the gospel, we join Jesus in dismantling systemic injustices and supremacies of all sorts. To make a change, we must be vigilant and look for opportunities for liberation wherever we are. Jesus stood up and named his calling. As his followers and disciples, we must stand with him.

Prayer: Lord, we follow Jesus as he stands with the oppressed, the poor, the captive, and the brokenhearted. Help us always to look for places to shine the light of liberation. In Jesus' name, Amen.

Rejoice and Blossom

Read Isaiah 35:1–10

The wilderness and the dry land shall be glad,
the desert shall rejoice and blossom;
like the crocus it shall blossom abundantly,
and rejoice with joy and singing...They shall see the glory of the Lord,
the majesty of our God. (Isaiah 35:1, 2a, 2c)

In my leadership role, I am often asked, "So, what are you going to do about the decline in mainline Christianity?" By decline, people mean that there are fewer members in their own congregations, less money, and well, things just aren't the same anymore. There is no "magic bullet" that I or anyone else can concoct that "fixes" this issue wholesale. I believe that our dryness is not a physical one, but a spiritual one. When we lack scriptural literacy, when we do not see spiritual practices as vital parts of our Christian walk, when we are comfortable with just doing things how they've always been done, we have shut off the necessary nourishing of God's spirit that is vital for growth and life.

The first signs of blossoming and rejuvenation are among us. As we stretch our spiritual roots down deep to connect with God, and connect with each other, we are building capacity and grace for new life among us. Grounding ourselves in spiritual disciplines of prayer and scriptural reflection, we can build new paths to connect and make room for new shoots to appear. It is a new world, and we are called forth to rejoice and blossom as we lean in to bring about God's new reign.

Prayer: Lord, give us the vision to see the desert in bloom, and the courage to rejoice even now. May the Holy Way be made known to all who seek you, and may everlasting joy be upon our heads. Amen.

Be Patient

Read James 5:7–10

Be patient, therefore, beloved, until the coming of the Lord. The farmer waits for the precious crop from the earth, being patient with it until it receives the early and the late rains. You also must be patient. Strengthen your hearts, for the coming of the Lord is near. (James 5:7–8)

The last thing most of us want to hear are the words "just be patient." We didn't like to hear it as children, and for me, patience is a hard thing to cultivate as an adult. I am a "fierce urgency of now" person. The last thing we want to hear is to be patient in suffering. Dr. King admonished the white moderates who tried to tell him that now was simply not the time to agitate for justice. When we are suffering, how can we patient? Why be patient? Who gets to tell me to be patient?

Just as waiting is not an inert activity, so the practice of patience must not be either. While we are waiting for God to move, to come, we must already be engaged in the work of ministry to and with one another. If we just stand still and do nothing to move the needle, patience can strip us bare. Standing still without spiritual activity can entrench suffering and deplete us. When impatience tries to overtake you, focus on strengthening your heart, mind, and spirit so that you continue to make progress toward the new world we all imagine. God is yet moving, so let us not stand still.

Prayer: Lord, it is hard to be patient, to wait on you to move. Help us to remember that you are always moving, even if we can't see. Keep us focused on the movement we can make as we keep our eyes on you. In Jesus' name, Amen.

We Will Not Be Afraid

Read Isaiah 12:2-6

Surely God is my salvation;
I will trust, and will not be afraid,
for the Lord God is my strength and my might;
he has become my salvation. (Isaiah 12:2)

As I write at the beginning of the COVID-19 pandemic, fear is on our minds. As people of faith, we have spoken the words, "Fear not" to ourselves and countless others. But as the numbers of infections and deaths continue to rise, so does our anxiety. We have many responses to fear, and too often our response can be to throw aside wisdom and discretion in order to seek an immediate resolution. We must speak to ourselves to say that we will trust God, follow the guidelines, and we will not allow fear to cripple our judgment.

It is not reasonable to expect that we will never feel afraid. But because of Christ, we can live in ways that do not allow fear to control us. Part of the challenge of letting go of ways that no longer work is to move beyond the fear of change, of what will happen when we let go. The new cannot come until we have given it space to appear. Only by releasing our clenched hands can they be open to receive. By giving ourselves permission to change, and accepting the grace that God has already given to do so, we can move beyond fear to a freedom that will give wings to our prophetic imaginations.

Prayer: Lord, help me to trust and not be afraid. Allow me to release that which I hold too close so that I may receive all that you are ready to bring forth in my life. In faith we pray, Amen.

Peace Surpassing Understanding

Read Philippians 4:4–7

Do not worry about anything, but in everything by prayer and supplication with thanksgiving let your requests be made known to God. And the peace of God, which surpasses all understanding, will guard your hearts and your minds in Christ Jesus. (Philippians 4:6–7)

Growing up, I always wondered how I would know when I was experiencing the peace of God. As my grandma used to say, "just keep living!" The important part of this text is that it is peace that surpasses all understanding. When being OK in a situation doesn't seem to make sense, that's when I know that the peace of God is guarding my heart and mind in Christ Jesus.

Life throws constant obstacles in our paths. It is important to develop spiritual resources that will sustain us during those difficult seasons. By developing a lifestyle that includes spiritual practices, we can build up the resilience we need to shelter in the peace of God. One of the most exciting aspects of the peace of God is that it can be a powerful witness. I do not understand how people without spiritual resources are able to weather life's storms. But I do know that being kept in a state of peace in the midst of difficulty, while it is assuring, is also simply beyond my understanding. I'm not even sure if I am making sense with this explanation, but there you have it. The peace that surpasses all understanding is simply beyond my ability to explain. Thank you, God!

Prayer: Dear Lord, I praise you for the peace you give that defies explanation. I am grateful to be able to recognize your presence even when I don't understand. Let my soul continue to find rest and peace in you always. With a grateful heart we pray, Amen.

Our Help Is God

Read Psalm 146: 5-10

Happy are those whose help is the God of Jacob,
* whose hope is in the LORD their God,*
who made heaven and earth,
* the sea, and all that is in them;*
who keeps faith forever;
* who executes justice for the oppressed;*
* who gives food to the hungry. (Psalm 146:5–7)*

In the black church where I grew up, I learned to call on God for help, to acknowledge my need and to always be grateful for all that God had done, was doing, and would do. When calling to God for help, the gospel music of the black church has a particular message template: "Trouble, trouble, but God...." Another construction is: "Trouble, trouble, then God..." In other words, the pain and suffering of the community were named, along with the need, and the answer was always that God showed up, God provided, God delivered. I learned at an early age that I needed God.

Sometimes I fear that some of us don't need God. We are perhaps self-sufficient and don't understand the humble posture of acknowledging that God is our help, and that our hope must be in the Lord our God. While it is necessary to praise and worship God, there is a real sense in which we are creatures who need the Creator. To ignore that need is to miss out on being a witness to God's work on our behalf in the world. Yes, we have agency, but we are not God. Yes, we are intelligent, but we are not God. I know I need God, and I invite you to acknowledge your need for God's help and hope.

Prayer: O God, our help in ages past, our hope for years to come, our shelter from the stormy blast, and our eternal home. We need you, dear Lord, and we acknowledge that our hope is in you alone. Amen.

Pray without Ceasing

Read 1 Thessalonians 5:16–24

Rejoice always, pray without ceasing, give thanks in all circumstances; for this is the will of God in Christ Jesus for you. (1 Thessalonians 5:16–18)

As children, we learned to fold our hands and bow our heads in prayer. We learned the Lord's Prayer. We learned to say prayers at bedtime, giving thanks for family, friends, and the seemingly small desires of childhood. I remember having to give a sentence prayer at the close of Sunday school, and thinking hard about what I would say. (I was determined not to say, "Jesus wept.") When I was in college, I went forward to kneel at the altar for prayer for the first time. Homesick and on my own, I remember thinking, "this is what they were trying to teach me." When they taught me to pray, they knew that someday I would need to be able to do it alone.

Praying without ceasing is not so much a matter of frequency. It is rather an understanding that we need to be in constant relationship with God through prayer. Prayers of joy, prayers of thanksgiving, prayers for direction and wisdom, prayers of lament and grief, prayers in sacred silence—all prayer connects us to God. With such connection, the prophetic imagination can soar, and we have strength to follow God's lead into the new world of God's reign.

Prayer: O Holy One, whether on our knees or with eyes wide open, whether in silence or fervent petition, keep us close to you in prayer, and help us to hear your voice. In Jesus' name, Amen.

Fourth Week of Advent

The One of Peace

Read Micah 5:2–5a

And he shall stand and feed his flock in the strength of the LORD,
in the majesty of the name of the LORD his God.
And they shall live secure, for now he shall be great
to the ends of the earth;
and he shall be the one of peace. (Micah 5:4–5a)

Leadership consultants and therapists commonly write about the importance of being a "non-anxious presence," or being "the adult in the room," as a sign of leadership. When the stakes are high, leaders understand that how they respond may well determine the dynamics in the room, and the success or failure of the endeavor. Peace is not the absence of conflict, but rather the presence of respect and order in the process.

According to the prophet Micah, the one who will be born in Bethlehem will be "the one of peace" (Micah 5:5a). Whether as a ruler or a shepherd, the Messiah will be the one to ensure security and peace. As followers of Jesus Christ, we too can be the non-anxious presence in a room. As a teacher, Jesus used the ordinary elements of daily life to teach eternal truths. He found ways to help others come into their own understanding without violating the dignity of their own experiences. By including those on the margins, Jesus was always the adult in the room, never yielding to racist or misogynistic patterns in his community. He modeled a new way of community, teaching us how to model the kin[g]dom of God. The new world will require us to be the ones of peace, the adults in the room.

Prayer: O God, may we be instruments of your peace in every space we inhabit. May the example of Jesus be written on our hearts as we show up in the world in new ways. With the peace of Christ, we pray in Jesus' name, Amen.

Restore Us, O God

Read Psalm 80:1–7

Restore us, O God;
let your face shine that we may be saved. (Psalm 80:3)

As I write, the COVID-19 global pandemic is settling in, with no end in sight. We celebrated Easter virtually across the world, an Easter unlike any in history. Many of us long to return to our previous patterns and rhythms of life. But it is becoming clear to me that the world has already forever changed. There is no returning to the way it was. And that is a good thing. As church, we no longer have a choice to adopt change or not. We must adapt or cease to be.

The exiled and oppressed nation of Israel cried out for a leader who would restore what they had known. The message of Jesus was nothing like what had been before. His birth upended expectations, and his ministry, death, and resurrection introduced disruptions of all sorts. Out of those disruptions, the church of Jesus Christ was formed and shaped. In this time, a new disruption has now reshaped the world in which we minister and proclaim God's good news. We must respond in ways previously unimaginable, asking God to restore our determination to be a movement for wholeness in a yet fragmented world.

Prayer: Gracious God, restore us not to what has been, but to a fervor and determination to reflect your love in new ways. We look forward as we follow Christ, Amen.

God Who Is Able

Read Romans 16:25–27

Now to God who is able to strengthen you according to my gospel and the proclamation of Jesus Christ,... (Romans 16:25a)

Everything about my faith begins with what I believe about God. My faith is not vested in whether God does or does not do what I ask. For me, my faith is grounded in what I believe God is able to do. And for me, that is everything. As the angel spoke to Mary, "for with God, nothing shall be impossible." I believe this because I cannot accept limits placed on a God who is beyond my knowing. It is not up to you or me or any other created being to set limits on or diminish God's ability or love.

As we consider how God is leading and guiding the followers of Jesus Christ to imagine how church must show up to respond and live into a new world, we must do so with a clear understanding that God is able. There are no limits on that ability. Because of Christ, we enter into a fullness of relationship with God that can usher in not only love and peace but also mercy and justice. I can only respond to such an opportunity with praise for God, faith in Jesus Christ, and excitement for my fellow believers traveling this road in this season.

Prayer: Now to God who is able to strengthen us, to the only wise God, through Jesus Christ, to whom be the glory forever, Amen.

Teach Me Your Paths

Read Psalm 25:1–10

Make me to know your ways, O Lord;
*   teach me your paths.*
Lead me in your truth, and teach me,
*   for you are the God of my salvation;*
*   for you I wait all day long. (Psalm 25:4–5)*

Jesus' prayer for his disciples in John 17 centers around his desire that his followers would come to have a relationship with God as he did. That relationship was characterized by a consistent prayer life and knowledge of the Scriptures. With a similar heartfelt desire, the psalmist prays to God for a relationship in which God would make God's ways known; God is invited to teach and lead.

One of the most powerful aspects of Christian community is our collective work to know more of God. Studying the Scriptures together gives us the benefit of one another's discernment and reflection, stretching and inviting one another to grow. Recognizing that God speaks to us in different ways, we must respect the variety of gifts God uses among us to teach us. It is our own spiritual work that gives us the discernment to determine whether we find ourselves in the midst of those who are theologically grounded.

From this ongoing learning and engagement, our spirits are strengthened and we can embrace the permission that God has already given for us to show up in the world in new ways, nourished and equipped to live in covenant with God and all of creation.

Prayer: Dear Lord, we lift up our souls to you for nourishment and sustenance. Teach us, and lead us that we might know you moIt isre, and live into our callings faithfully. In Jesus' name, we pray, Amen.

Faithful or Clueless?

Read Matthew 1:18–25

Her husband Joseph, being a righteous man and unwilling to expose her to public disgrace, planned to dismiss her quietly. But just when he had resolved to do this, an angel of the Lord appeared to him in a dream and said, "Joseph, son of David, do not be afraid to take Mary as your wife, for the child conceived in her is from the Holy Spirit." (Matthew 1:19–20)

The story of Jesus' birth is actually a messy one. A teenage girl is engaged to be married. In a strange twist of events, she discovers she is pregnant, although still a virgin. The "father" is the Holy Spirit. That story didn't play well in the first century, and it would not play well now. Given the certain social disgrace (not to mention certain death for Mary), Joseph's response is positively noble and compassionate. On the other hand, Joseph's choice could be seen as foolish and irresponsible. In either case, Mary would bear the brunt of society's disdain, as women have for centuries.

Is Joseph faithful, or just clueless? Is he being given a line or is he sincerely called to participate in this narrative out of love and care? Whether you affirm the virgin birth or not, Mary and Joseph entered into marriage on the wrong side of the law and society. If Mary and Joseph had not been willing to act in the midst of society's disapproval, this story would have had a different ending. We honestly don't know all the details of what happened, but the reality would likely have been even messier.

It's hard to know what mixture of societal and personal disdain those who have the courage to imagine might face. As we celebrate the birth of Jesus, it is worth reminding ourselves that his story, like so many of ours, was messy. And God used it for God's glory.

Prayer: God of love, we know that we may find ourselves at odds with society when we follow your path. Comfort us when your call takes messy paths. Lead us, guide us always is our prayer. Amen.

Preparing the Way for Jesus

Read Luke 3:7–18

"I baptize you with water; but one who is more powerful than I is coming; I am not worthy to untie the thong of his sandals. He will baptize you with the Holy Spirit and fire." (Luke 3:16)

One of the primary tenets of journalism is that the reporter should never become the story. A reporter remains outside the narrative, asking clarifying questions to highlight the significance of the story. When it becomes apparent that a journalist cares more about her own ratings than the story, credibility can be lost.

Scripture reminds us in many places that a voice in the wilderness was prophesied who would be on the scene before Jesus to prepare his way. Anticipation for the Messiah was so high that people were hungry for John's message. He did in fact have his own disciples—among them, Andrew, Peter's brother. But John fulfills his role with great integrity. He does not seek his own spotlight, and continually reminds the people that someone is coming who is greater than he. He offers insightful teaching that engages many followers. Even Jesus comes to him to be baptized. John is so effectively disruptive to the power structures that Herod the ruler seeks to imprison him.

As we share the good news in our comings and goings, it is important that we ourselves not become the story. It is human nature to form connections with those to whom we can easily relate, and as with John, there are those who will be drawn to a given leader for many reasons. But the moment we become the story, we diminish the good news. We must always be preparing the way for Jesus.

Prayer: Lord, may the words of my mouth and the meditations of my heart always point the way to Jesus. Amen.

The Lord God Is in Our Midst

Read Zephaniah 3:14–20

The LORD, your God, is in your midst,
a warrior who gives victory;
he will rejoice over you with gladness,
he will renew you in his love;
he will exult over you with loud singing. (Zephaniah 3:17)

And so now God has broken through the heavens to be in our midst. God has taken the form of humanity to reveal Godself through Jesus. From the centuries of longing for a deliverer, to the realities of a messy story that defies explanation, we are left with the reality of a suffering servant, a gentle, loving and powerful advocate who disrupts systems and calls people forth into new ways of communion with God. As he teaches, there are many for whom his presence and ministry are threats to systems that have given them platform and power, perhaps for too long.

God is in our midst, surrounding us with love and peace. We are challenged to love one another as Jesus loved us, beyond even the love we have for ourselves. Oh, how we want to be renewed, and in the midst of such love and presence, we walk boldly into the vision God gives for us to lead and shape a new world. The kin[g]dom of God must yet arise to proclaim the good news, and deliver those who are poor, captive, and brokenhearted. There is so much for us to learn; so much God has to teach us still.

Prayer: Loving and faithful God, thank you that you are always with us. Give us courage to imagine not only a new world, but the church we must be in it. Give us grace as we change and free us from the fears that would limit our vision. We are confident that you will complete the work you have given us to do. Amen.

Advent Candle Services

Week 1 – HOPE

1 Corinthians 1:3-9

Reader 1: Today we celebrate the first Sunday of Advent, and we light the candle of Hope. In a world too often filled with uncertainty and anxiety, we rejoice in the hope that we have in Jesus Christ. In 1 Corinthians 1:3-9, we hear the gratitude and hope that Paul has in God, and in the gift of Jesus.

Reader 2: (*reads 1 Corinthians 1:3-9*)

Reader 3: Advent is a time of anticipation, when we remember how the expectant hope of the world was fulfilled in the coming of Jesus, and how we lay claim to the hope that we have in Christ every day. Through Christ, God promises to strengthen us as we live into the call to be Jesus' disciples.

Reader 4: We find our hope also in the Scriptures, where we read in 1 Corinthians 3:9 – "God is faithful." May our hearts lay hold to this hope today and every day and may the light of this candle remind us of God's enduring faithfulness.

(The Hope candle is lit.)

Prayer: Our hope is in you, Lord. Fill us with the hope you give, the hope that sustains us and gives us strength for the days ahead; the hope that does not disappoint. In Jesus' name we pray. Amen.

SONG: *suggested: When God is a Child – verse 1*

Week 2 – PEACE

Isaiah 11:1-10

Reader 1: Today we celebrate the 2nd Sunday of Advent, and we light the candle of Peace. The famous image of the "peaceable kingdom" shows animals who are natural enemies lying down together in peace. In Isaiah 11:1-10, we hear the prophet Isaiah speak to Israel about who the Messiah will be:

Reader 2: (*reads Isaiah 11:1-10*)

Reader 3: God says that the Messiah will be filled with the Spirit of the Lord, that he will not judge by what his eyes see or what his ears hear. Jesus was to come to us in righteousness and faithfulness, to bring a world where all have enough. In such a world, there can be peace.

Reader 4: When the Spirit of the Lord fills us, we can have peace, and our movement for wholeness will be grounded in justice and faithfulness. We thank God for this vision for our movement as we light the candle of peace.

(The Peace candle is lit.)

Prayer: We receive your Spirit, O God, that our hearts might be filled with your righteousness and faithfulness. May we see and hear with your wisdom and your peace, and may our work together serve to bring your reign of peace to pass. In Christ's name we pray. Amen.

SONG: *suggested: When God is a Child – verse 2*

Week 3 – LOVE

Isaiah 61:1-4, 8-11

Reader 1: Today, on this third Sunday of Advent, we light the candle of love. It is because God loved us so very much that we celebrate the coming of God's Son to be among us. The love that God calls us to is a love that works to affirm humanity, to dismantle oppression, to liberate those bound by oppression. Let us hear the text that Jesus read from Isaiah in his home synagogue, the text that he declared as his own mission:

Reader 2: *(reads Isaiah 61:1-4, 8-11)*

Reader 3: Jesus taught his disciples in John 15 that they should love one another as he had loved them so that the world would know they were his disciples. This continues to be our call—to love courageously, completely, creatively, so that the world can see who Jesus is.

Reader 4: 1 John 3:18 says, "let us love, not in word or speech, but in truth and action." As we light the candle of Love, let us commit to choosing every day to love in truth and action. May we always reflect the limitless, boundless love of God in all we do.

(The Love candle is lit (pink candle)).

Prayer: God of love, help us to reflect your love, help us to love courageously and completely, through our actions to ensure that all humanity may flourish because of your great love for us all. Thank you for the example you gave in Jesus Christ; may we love as he has loved us. May it be so. Amen.

SONG: *suggested: When God is a Child – verse 3*

Week 4 – JOY

Luke 1:46b-55

Reader 1: Today is the 4th Sunday of Advent, and we light the candle of joy. We are reminded that joy can be present in the midst of uncertainty, for joy comes from the fullness of God's presence among us, given through the one we call Jesus the Christ. Mary, his mother, responded from a heart full of joy when she learned she would be the mother of Jesus:

Reader 2: *(reads Luke 1:46b-55)*

Reader 3: Like Mary, we rejoice in what God has done, how God has provided, the justice that comes when love and mercy work with justice, the satisfying in our souls that brings a smile to our face despite circumstances. Joy, joy, God's great joy—let us light this candle. May its light cast out darkness, reminding us that the joy of the Lord is our strength,

Prayer: We open our hearts to receive from you, O Holy One, the peace that passes all understanding and the fulness of joy that cannot be taken away from us. May your Spirit and the love you gave through Jesus continue to fill our cups to overflowing with joy, now and always, In the name of Jesus we pray. Amen.

SONG: *suggested: When God is a Child – verse 4*

CHRIST CANDLE

Luke 2:1-20

Reader 1: *(reads Luke 2:1-20)*

Reader 2: Our God is with Emmanuel, God has torn through the heavens and come down, as the prophet Isaiah prayed. Oh, how we are rejoicing! Just as the shepherds and angels bore witness to the great thing that God was doing among them in the birth of the Christ Child, so we must continue to tell and share the wonderful things that God is doing in our midst today.

Reader 3: In Matthew 2, we are reminded that Jesus was also to be called "Emmanuel", meaning "God with us." God's faithfulness is great; God's mercies are new every morning. Jesus has come, Jesus died, was resurrected, and we are called each day to rejoice in the completed work of Jesus Christ. The shadow of the cross was visible on the manger, and we stand here rejoicing in the powerful story of love and resurrection, even as we celebrate the birth of the Christ Child.

Reader 4: As we light the Christ Candle, we are ever mindful that Christ's presence comes to dispel darkness, to bring hope, to establish peace, to reflect God's love, and to fill us with joy. As we light the Christ Candle today, may the presence of our Lord and Savior be with each of us, now and always, helping us to imagine and build the new world he has called us to create.

Prayer: Thank you, God, for your great love, in sending Jesus to be Emmanuel, to be God with us. May the presence of Christ be seen in us, and may we work to bring Christ's presence to a world so in need of your love. With our hearts full of love, joy and gratitude, we pray in Christ's name. Amen.